Read & Resp[...]

FOR
KS2

Read & Respond

FOR KS2

Author: Celia Warren

Development Editor: Simret Brar

Editor: Margaret Eaton

Assistant Editor: Vicky Butt

Series Designer: Anna Oliwa

Designer: Q2A Media

Illustrations: Paul Howard

Text © 2008 Celia Warren © 2008 Scholastic Ltd

Designed using Adobe InDesign

Published by Scholastic Ltd, Villiers House,
Clarendon Avenue, Leamington Spa,
Warwickshire CV32 5PR
www.scholastic.co.uk

Printed by Bell & Bain
1 2 3 4 5 6 7 8 9   8 9 0 1 2 3 4 5 6 7

British Library Cataloguing-in-Publication Data
A catalogue record for this book is available from the British
Library.
ISBN 978-1407-10003-6

Acknowledgements

The publishers gratefully acknowledge permission to reproduce
the following copyright material: **The Economist Newspaper
Limited** for the use and adaptation of an article 'Pigged out'
(opinion leader) from *The Economist* of 11th January 1998 ©
1998, The Economist Newspaper Limited, London 11th January
1998 (1998, The Economist). **The Random House Group Ltd**
for the use of extracts from *Pig-heart Boy* by Malorie Blackman
© 1997, Oneta Malorie Blackman (1997, Doubleday). Every
effort has been made to trace copyright holders for the works
reproduced in this book, and the publishers apologise for any
inadvertent omissions.

Pig-heart Boy

About the book

Pig-heart Boy was first published in 1997 at a time when research into the possibility of xenotransplantation of animal organs to human recipients, was at its height. Although such an operation has never happened, towards the end of the last century this procedure seemed to be distinctly plausible. The medical side of the story described by Malorie Blackman in *Pig-heart Boy* is well researched to ensure credibility.

Although medical research has moved on since the book was first published, there is still a shortage of donor organs and there remain ethical dilemmas over the means of helping seriously ill patients.

Plot summary

Thirteen-year-old Cameron Kelsey, desperately needs a new heart if he is to live longer than a few more months. His diseased heart has left him weak and unable to join in normal activities with his friends, and it seems unlikely that a suitable human donor heart will become available in time. Cam especially misses being able to swim with his friends and play their favourite home-spun diving game, Daredevil Dive.

Meanwhile, Cam's parents are always arguing – and it's always about him. He is watching his family fall apart and missing his Nan (who lives 200 miles away), when suddenly Dr Bryce comes along with a possible solution: a procedure where Cam's heart will be replaced with a pig's heart, from a genetically modified pig.

Although there are many risks involved, Cam and his parents decide to go ahead with the operation – but his life afterwards is far from straightforward. The reactions of his friends –

and the general public – when the news is leaked to the newspapers after the operation, force Cameron and his parents to face a number of difficult issues dealt with in the book. The ethics of xenotransplantation focus on one among many issues, including prejudice, friendship, loyalty, disloyalty, wealth, poverty, honesty, life values, bullying, extremism, animal experimentation.

The open ending of the book provides space for optimism, and will leave young readers with many thought-provoking issues and an increased awareness of the many dilemmas people can face in life.

About the author

Malorie Blackman, who has written over 50 books, has a reputation for writing powerful stories that never shy away from controversial and topical issues. Her first book was *Not So Stupid!*, published in 1990.

As well as her many books, she has written scripts for television (including episodes of *Byker Grove* and *Whizziwig*) plus a play, *The Amazing Birthday*, performed at the Polka Theatre in 2002. Other books include the award-winning *Noughts and Crosses* series, *Jessica Strange*, *Hacker*, *A.N.T.I.D.O.T.E* and *Dangerous Reality*.

Malorie lives with her husband and daughter in Kent.

> **Facts and figures**
> First published by Doubleday in 1997. Among other awards it was shortlisted for the 1998 Carnegie Medal. It was adapted into a Bafta award-winning TV serial in 2000 (Best children's drama).

Guided reading

Chapter 1

Pig-heart Boy is divided into chapters, grouped under the headings 'Cause', 'Effect' and 'Consequences'. This first chapter, headed 'Consequences', seems out of sequence. The entire chapter is in italics, representing inner dialogue. It is subtitled 'Dying' – but can a first-person narrator write about his own death?

Advise the children to keep this passage in mind, as they continue through the book. They will find pointers as to who Alex is, and so on. It sets the tone for the story's 'life and death' nature. Clues to interpreting 'Now for the hard part… Now for the easy part…' will appear as the children read on.

Chapters 2–3

The narrative continues in chronological order, Cameron introducing other characters as readers progress through the book. Cam's efforts to control his own life begin immediately and graphically at the bottom of the pool.

Discuss the use of language. Discuss the single-word lines in the opening paragraph. What is their purpose? (Added contrast to 'the noise'.) Encourage the children to read the last line of Chapter 2 aloud. How does the text layout affect how it is read and its purpose? (It speeds it up – representing time running out; rising heart-rate.)

Invite the children to locate the frequent use of figurative expressions ('a new track on an old CD'; 'hit the roof'), including similes, such as 'stomach… churning like a liquidiser', 'beads of sweat… like hot needles'. Ask the children to find pointers to Cam's relationship with his parents. (They knock on his door; he flinches at his mother's slap.)

Invite the children to explain why Daredevil Dive is capitalised. (It is an invented game – the formal name elevates its status.) Challenge them to consider how Cam's feelings are shown through (a) description ('leaned against one wall and looked down'), and (b) direct speech, such as how he reveals his presence by shouting 'Stop it!'

Chapter 4

The similes continue: 'Her voice chilled like liquid nitrogen' (explain nitrogen's intensely cold properties, liquefying at nearly –200°C). Compare this with the previous chapter when Mum's voice 'burnt like a laser'. (Her moods change!) Examine how Cam's joke eases the tension. He cannot understand why his laughter suddenly turns to tears. Invite the children to find clues: a long-standing emotional situation, sudden release of pent-up feelings, more than one factor (parental arguments; fear and pain; bullying; restrictions on normal living – an accumulation of worries suddenly confronted).

Ask the children about 'Dad's saccharine smile' (an artificial sweetener). Compare 'sugary smile' or 'sweet smile'. Does 'saccharine' imply that Dad's smile is forced? Why? (He is trying to be positive against all odds.) Draw attention to the paragraph beginning 'I watched Dr Bryce carefully'. The dip into passive tense reinforces the doctor's detachment. Ensure that the children notice Cam's closing words: 'It's quite simple, really…' – recognised by his best friend, Marlon, in the next chapter, as Cameron's catchphrase, exemplifying his viewpoint.

Help the children to define 'crucial' and 'prevarication' from the context.

Chapters 5–6

Dialogue carries much of the plot here. Invite comments on how this affects the pace and heightens reader involvement. Identify more graphic imagery, such as 'things… felt like molten lava'. Examine how the author uses description effectively to show Cam's numbed reaction to the transplant confirmation. Many sentences begin with 'I', focusing attention on the character. Ask what the doctors' mutual use of first names reveals. (They enjoy a close professional partnership.)

Examine the common root of 'xenograft' and 'xenotransplant' (*xeno* is a Greek word

Guided reading

meaning strange or stranger). Introduce the word/concept 'xenophobia'. (A fear of anything strange or foreign.) Despite Mum's pregnancy, Cam describes a 'disintegrating' family. Can the children identify pointers to justify his view, which is often revealed through dialogue and body language?

Chapters 7–9

These three chapters, titled 'Talking', 'The Announcement' and 'Messages' have a common theme of communication (and miscommunication). The dialogue reveals more of Cam's relationship with his parents. Look at the word 'optimist' and how Cam uses 'sad specimen' rather than 'pessimist'. (This is an example of the author's periodical use of humour to relieve tension.) Compare Cam's initial description of a heart transplant with the modified tone of his second speech. What does it reveal about the character's feelings? These chapters illuminate various experiences of embarrassment – including Cam's 'naff poem'.

Chapter 10

Stilted conversation (Cam and Mum) and displacement activity (Dad) create touching humour to a tense situation. How is this achieved so realistically? (Note the unfinished and half-sentences.) Help the children to compare the parents' behaviour with earlier examples (see Chapter 4) where the roles of doubting are reversed.

Chapters 11–14

These three chapters represent the anticipation, actuality and aftermath of Cam's hospitalisation. Encourage the children to examine the content of Cam's (italicised) webcam monologues in the light of his comment that the unborn Alex is a 'great listener'. Compare Cam's changed phraseology and style when he is speaking to his parents or his doctor. Encourage empathy. Ask

the children: *How are we different when we are with different people?*

Help the children to identify how the term 'ECG' (ElectroCardioGram) is derived, and why. (It is a shorter, easier term to use.) Highlight the increasingly adventurous figurative expressions ('My stomach feels as if…').

Encourage the children to examine the journalistic language and layout in the *Daily Press*, identifying fact, fiction and conjecture. Ask them to look for indicators of who provided the true bits (for example, the use of Cam's catchphrase to sound plausible).

Chapter 15

The first under the heading 'Effect', this chapter is a pivotal point in the plot, when Cam has to face life with his new pig heart and the knowledge that the secret is out. It deals very much with expectations – of Cam, his parents, his friends, the crowds, the police, the medics. Invite the children to look for areas of hope versus confrontation.

Chapters 16–19

Invite the children to observe how feelings and action are continually interwoven, through graphic description, inner dialogue and direct speech. The use of imagery continues, such as 'I had furious, charging elephants in my stomach'. The temptation of wealth adds a fresh strand to the numerous issues covered in this book, with the reference to 'love of money (being) the root of all evil' (a biblical quotation). Ask the children to compare what Cam says to his parents on the subject with what he says to Alex via the camcorder.

Prejudice, fear through ignorance, embarrassment, anger and resentment all figure in these chapters – none more so than in Cam's return to school. Invite the children to observe how the author makes the classroom situation so emotionally charged. Draw attention to how the reader realises before Cam does how Julia is

Guided reading

going to react, helping to increase the sympathy felt towards the protagonist.

Chapter 20

The understated title 'Nan' heralds this character's importance in Cam's life. Remind the children how, in Chapter 5, we learn of Cam's regret that she lives 200 miles away. Encourage them to re-read that early paragraph. Ask the children: *In what ways does Nan help to smooth over 'complications'?* (She is practical, kind, caring, down-to-earth, loving – encourage the children to look for textual evidence.) Ask them to note the acronym, LEPAR, of the fictional animal rights group. What does this bring to mind? (Lepers and their unclean, socially excluded, status in biblical times.)

Chapter 21

Personal freedoms are further explored, together with changes in Cam's personality. Invite the children to look at the emotively charged shades of meaning and us of near-synonyms during Cam's conversation with Andrew (pushy, confident, arrogant, sure of/full of oneself). Observe how the author creates a happy atmosphere, friendships restored, and a sense of normality returning to Cam's life. How does this add to the impact of the woman protestor's act? Encourage the children to consider labels: weirdo, peanut head, pig-heart boy, murderer. Compare those that are malicious with those that are not – complete with Nan's anger-defusing and humorous 'a couple of eggs short of the full breakfast'.

Chapters 22–24

Discuss why Cam repeats 'I am not going to cry' and why he is untruthful in his answers to Dr Bryce. Ask the children why thinking of Alex might 'hurt'. (Cam's fear of dying before his sibling arrived; wistful longing for the security of babyhood?)

Chapter 24 ends with the words 'I knew I wasn't going to make it' and the following chapter is the first of the next 'Consequences' section. Invite the children to re-read Chapter 1 at this point. How much easier is this to interpret now? (Was it a near-death experience? Is the author offering a choice of endings?) Compare 'Cause' and 'Effect' (both singular) with 'Consequences' (plural). Does the 'easy bit'/'hard bit' relate to both living *and* dying? (Neither option is easy, both are hard.) Ask the children to keep these ideas in mind as they continue reading.

Chapters 25–27

The remaining 'Consequences' chapters see the death of Nan, but not before she has shared words of wisdom and encouragement with Cam. The book ends with a final webcam message to Alex, and readers learn that Dr Bryce's second pig-heart transplant patient has died. The webcam message combines realistic expectations with optimism as Cam declares that living long enough to welcome Alex into the world is his next challenge. Ask the children in what ways Cam's closing words ('signing off') could be interpreted.

Shared reading

Extract 1

● Encourage the children to infer the relationship between Cam and Marlon through close reading of this text from Chapter 5. Underline examples of Cam's facial and body language speaking for him ('smile tugging…', 'shrugged', 'Eyebrows raised, I tilted my head…'). Ask the children: *How well do the boys know each other, when they don't need words?*

● Highlight examples of colloquialisms, such as 'nuts', 'round the twist' and 'digging and digging'. Explain to the children that expressions like these help dialogue sound natural and establish characters.

● Point out the punctuation of dialogue, including the inset text. Ask the children to examine how the author often avoids using tag-words, writing a descriptive statement to indicate the speaker: 'Marlon couldn't believe his ears', 'Marlon raised his right hand'. Highlight the punctuation marks relating to direct speech.

● Circle examples of rhetorical questions, such as 'What do *you* think?'. Encourage the children to read this line aloud, recognising the need to place stress on the word 'you'. Similarly: 'Why would anyone ask me *that*?', 'But suppose *they* find out?'

Extract 2

● Highlight emotive words and statements containing value judgments, designed to influence the reader and sensationalise the event, such as: 'exclusively reveal', 'waves of controversy', 'guinea pig on the frontiers of medicine'.

● Underline examples of blatant inaccuracies and inconsistencies. Ask the children: *What do these suggest about the nature of the article?* (Parts are made up, including direct 'quotations' falsely attributed to Cam and members of his family; the name of his school – a 13-year-old is not at primary school, although earlier he is called a 'teenager' and his age wrongly given as 14.) Examples such as these suggest a journalist writing in haste, not caring about factual content so much as sensationalism.

● Point out the layout of the text. How does 'continued on page 4' help the plot? (It speeds up the narrative while indicating the level of media coverage.)

● What does the author achieve through including the article? (It foreshadows what Cameron will face when he returns to home and school.)

Extract 3

● Explain how the italic font distinguishes this monologue from the main narrative and how the word 'Me!' in regular font, amidst italics, indicates stress.

● Underline colloquialisms in this example of Cam's webcam soliloquies: 'It's me again', 'Bring them on', 'stuffed envelopes into my hand'.

● Highlight rhetorical questions: 'And guess what?', 'Can you imagine?'.

● Together, locate figurative expressions: 'didn't put a foot wrong', 'hit the roof', 'went absolutely ballistic'. Ask what these indicate about Cam's state of mind and mood. (He is buoyant but contemplative, rationalising his reactions and behaviour through conversational reasoning: 'All I could see', 'of course', 'I can't believe…', 'I still don't…', 'I shouldn't have…'.)

● Ask the children what is implied in the last paragraph, beginning 'I think I'll shut up now…'. Does this mean that Cam has modified his views? Has he calmed down? Is he ready to face his family?

Extract 1

'Are you nuts? Are you completely round the twist?' Marlon couldn't believe his ears.

I didn't answer. I bit back the smile tugging at the corners of my mouth.

'You're not going to do it, are you?'

'What d'you think?' I replied.

Marlon stared at me. 'I don't know,' he said at last. 'I... I'm sorry I reacted like that. It's just that... you took me by surprise.'

I shrugged, then added quickly, 'But this is between you and me, right? You're not to tell anyone, not your sister, not Rashid and Andrew, not even your mum and dad. Promise?'

'I promise.' Marlon raised his right hand. 'What're you going to tell everyone – after it's over?'

'I'll tell them I had a heart transplant – which will be true.'

'And what happens when people ask where the heart came from?'

'Why would anyone ask me that? And besides, if they do, I'll just say a suitable donor was found at the last minute. And I was lucky enough to get the heart.'

'But from a pig!'

'No one will know that – unless you tell them.'

'No, I won't,' Marlon denied quickly. 'But isn't it bound to come out?'

'I don't see why. Dr Bryce said that after the transplant he'd wait six months before announcing it to the media, and even then, he wouldn't tell them my name.'

'But suppose they find out? The newspapers and the TV have ways of digging and digging until—'

'Whoa! We're getting a little ahead of ourselves here. Dr Bryce hasn't even chosen me yet. He said he'd get in touch with Mum and Dad at the end of the week to let them know his decision.'

'D'you want it to be you?'

Eyebrows raised, I tilted my head to one side as I regarded my friend.

'I'm sorry. I guess it is a silly question,' Marlon mumbled.

Text © 1997, Oneta Malorie Blackman.

Extract 2

DAILY PRESS

WORLD EXCLUSIVE!

THE BOY WITH A PIG'S HEART INSIDE HIS BODY!

TODAY THE DAILY PRESS CAN EXCLUSIVELY REVEAL THAT CAMERON KELSEY (ABOVE), AGED 14 OF LARKIN ROAD, DEALWORTH IN LONDON HAS MADE MEDICAL HISTORY.

In a dramatic twelve hour operation sure to send waves of controversy around the world, the heart of a pig has been transplanted into the body of Cameron Kelsey. With time running out for the sick child, and no likely prospect of a human donor, the only hope seemed to be eminent surgeon and immunologist Dr Richard Bryce. His pioneering techniques for overcoming rejection between species have opened the way for a new wave of transplants between animals and man.

Cameron Kelsey, the teenager from Dealworth, is remarkably cool about being a guinea pig on the frontiers of medicine. Asked about the special problems of using a pig-heart, he said, "It's simple really. The only thing I have to be careful about now is taking my medicine to stop my body rejecting my new heart." His mother Catherine said, "Cameron knows the risks, he knows that he faces a lifetime of check-ups and anti-rejection drugs, but all he can talk about is going swimming and playing football." Cameron's heart was damaged beyond repair by a viral infection two years ago, and his life ever since has been a slow decline punctuated by major crises. "When Dr Bryce approached us, it was a shock,

yes, but it was the chance for my son to lead a normal life. I leapt at the chance," said Mrs Kelsey.

Although the idea of transplantation from other species into humans has been discussed and debated for a few years now, this is the first time that such an operation has actually gone ahead. Dr Bryce has received media attention before when he first presented his opinion that the only way to overcome the shortage in human organs available for transplantation was to look at the organs of other species. No stranger to controversy, Dr Bryce has long sought to make his name – and his fortune – in this field.

Cameron Kelsey is known to be recovering in a private hospital and is thought to be doing well.

Friends close to the family told us that Cameron's parents allowed Cameron to make the final decision. After long and agonising deliberation, Cameron finally decided that he really had no other choice.

"It's simple really. I had to choose between living and dying – and I chose to live," said Cameron today. "And I'm feeling fine and fighting fit. I'd do the same thing again tomorrow!"

Cameron continued, "I can't wait to get back to school and start leading the life of a normal boy. I can't wait to swim and run and play football without getting breathless every two seconds."

Mrs Sola Shange, headmistress of Cameron's school, Ashmead Primary, said, "I knew that Cameron was in hospital for a transplant, but no, I didn't know...

continued on page 4

Text © 1997, Oneta Malorie Blackman.

Extract 3

Hi, Alex,

It's me again. We've just come back from a press conference. My first and last, I hope. Dr Bryce didn't put a foot wrong. I didn't put a foot right. Dr Bryce talked about me as if I was just a piece of machinery on an assembly line.

The first of many. Bring them on. Next!

That's how I felt when he was talking. But then, what did I expect? I don't know. Maybe I expected him to refer to me more. Maybe I expected him to refer to me less. Maybe I wanted to be special, unique. I don't know. All I know is, it was hot and bright under the lights and after a while I began to feel very sick. I was glad to get out of there. On the way out, two journalists stuffed envelopes into my hand. And guess what? Two newspapers offered me thousands and thousands for my story.

Me! Can you imagine?

But Mum and Dad said no and put the letters in the bin. I hit the roof. I mean, I went absolutely ballistic. All I could see was the money I was losing. It was as if they were stealing it out of my pocket – which of course they weren't. I can't believe how I blew up at them. I mean, I still don't see why we can't just take the money, give the papers a couple of interviews and laugh all the way to the bank, but I shouldn't have lost my temper like that. I don't know what came over me.

Yes, I do.

I think I became blinded by the pound signs in my eyes. It was a lot of money. Ah well! At least one day I'll be able to look back and say I was offered a fortune for my life story. Me! There's not many people who can say that!

I think I'll shut up now. I'm hungry. I'm going to go down for my dinner.

Talk to you soon!

Text © 1997, Oneta Malorie Blackman.

Plot, character and setting

Guesswork and knowledge

> **Objective:** To understand how writers use different structures to create coherence and impact.
> **What you need:** Copies of *Pig-heart Boy*, writing materials.

What to do
- Ask the children to read the first two chapters of *Pig-heart Boy*, pointing out the respective headings: 'Consequences' and 'Cause'. Invite the children to consider why the first chapter is out of sequence and the text in italics. Does Chapter 1 make sense in isolation?
- Divide the children into groups of about six to discuss and list the similarities and differences between the two chapters in terms of presentation, style and content. Ask them to look at tense (present; past), person (both: first), formatting (italics; regular font), setting. Compare levels of information and clarity. Do we know who Alex is and how s/he relates to the speaker? Do we know how characters introduced in Chapter 2 relate to the narrator?
- Discuss the content and contrasts of the two chapters as a class. Compare the titles 'Dying' and 'Ticking'. Ask the children: *Could someone write about their own death? Apart from a heart beat, what other connotations apply to 'ticking'?* (A clock; an unexploded bomb.)
- Invite the children to consider how the telling of the story would be affected if Chapter 2 had been the first chapter. (The impact of the opening scene would be reduced.)

> **Differentiation**
> **For older/more confident learners:** Challenge the children to write a few paragraphs answering the question: *How does Chapter 2 begin to shed light on the content of Chapter 1?*
> **For younger/less confident learners:** Ask the children to list briefly what is learned in the respective chapters, listing Chapter 1 as 'guesswork' and Chapter 2 as 'knowledge'.

Weighty words

> **Objective:** To understand underlying themes, causes and points of view.
> **What you need:** Copies of *Pig-heart Boy*, an enlarged copy of Extract 1 (page 8), photocopiable page 15, writing materials.

What to do
- Read Extract 1 together, annotating the text as you go through it. Encourage the children to infer traits of Cameron's and Marlon's characters and their friendship. Ask open questions, such as: *What suggests that Cameron totally trusts his best friend? How do we know that Marlon cares about Cameron's welfare?*
- Look especially at the words spoken by Marlon: 'But from a pig!' Invite the children to consider what exactly Marlon is saying. (For example: Is this wise? Isn't that disgusting? Have you really thought about the consequences? Might it be dangerous?) Based on the two characters' interaction, ask the children to decide if Marlon is likely to be showing concern for, or sitting in judgement on, Cameron.
- Hand out photocopiable page 15. Talk the children through the sample response, highlighting the textual references in Extract 1 to demonstrate how the children should approach their investigation of the text. Explain that they must support their decisions by close reference to the text.

> **Differentiation**
> **For older/more confident learners:** Ask the children to write a paragraph explaining how different experiences will influence Cameron's and Marlon's viewpoints on the subject of xenotransplantation.
> **For younger/less confident learners:** Invite the children to explain the reasons for their choices orally, scribing their reasons in note form.

Plot, character and setting

Communicating views

> **Objective:** To infer writers' perspectives from what
> is written and from what is implied.
> **What you need:** Copies of *Pig-heart Boy*,
> photocopiable page 16, writing materials.

What to do

● Explain that for authors to successfully present
situations and characters they must draw on
their own views and observations. Chapters 7
to 9 reveal both successes and breakdowns in
communication between characters. Ask: *Can
we safely infer that Malorie Blackman is aware of
problems in communication?*

● Note that chapter headings ('Talking', 'The
Announcement' and 'Messages'), point to
different forms of communication.

● Hand out copies of photocopiable page 16
so the children can write their findings as they
skim Chapters 7 to 9, noting examples of (a)
successful communication and (b) breakdowns
in communication. These won't always involve
words. (Talk through the example.)

● Based on their notes, ask what the children
consider to be the author's opinion of:
   ● family relationships
   ● some teachers.
Ask the children to use quotations from the book
and their notes to support their opinions as you
discuss this.

> **Differentiation**
> **For older/more confident learners:** Challenge
> the children to explain how and why Cam's
> communication differs with (a) his mother, (b) his
> teacher, and (c) his unborn sibling.
> **For younger/less confident learners:** Add quotations
> to the worksheet for the children to locate in the text.

Take heart!

> **Objective:** To distinguish between everyday use of
> words and their subject-specific use.
> **What you need:** Copies of *Pig-heart Boy*, writing
> materials.

What to do

● Allow the children five minutes to list as many
sayings and song titles that include the word
'heart' as they can. They might include: have
a heart, take heart, heartache, broken-hearted,
heart in one's mouth, downhearted.

● Now ask them to list words or expressions
relating to the organ in its biological sense: heart
beat, disease, by-pass, transplant, failure, attack.

● Read aloud Cameron's talk to the class in
Chapter 9. Compare the first half with the
second, after Mr Stewart's interruption, noting
the change in effect. Ask: *What was Cameron
trying to achieve at first, and why?* (Was he trying
to make a joke of his forthcoming operation? Or
perhaps he wanted to shock his teacher and peers
because he was angry and embarrassed?) *How did
his use of language achieve this?* (Graphic; lurid,
using words such as 'razor-sharp scalpel' and
'hacksaw' to sensationalise.) Invite individuals to
put these words into a different sentence without
causing distress (such as in a woodworking).

● Ask the children how Cam modifies the
second half of his talk, such as using softening
phrases: 'that's all' and 'think about it'.

● Return to the children's list of expressions.
Ask: *How do these expressions present the meaning
of 'heart' compared with its biological function?*

> **Differentiation**
> **For older/more confident learners:** Ask the children
> to define what the figurative expressions mean,
> reinforcing their distance from describing the heart
> as a functional muscle.
> **For younger/less confident learners:** Draw an
> outline of a large heart. Encourage the children to
> write 'biological' heart terms inside the outline and
> figurative expressions outside it.

Plot, character and setting

Style and structure

> **Objective:** To compare different types of narrative and information texts and identify how they are structured.
> **What you need:** Copies of *Pig-heart Boy*, photocopiable page 17, writing materials.

What to do

● Explain that *Pig-heart Boy* incorporates other styles of writing.
● Read the following quotations and ask the children to guess which styles they represent:

1. *'And look! I danced around for ages and I'm not even out of breath. So this is what it's like to be healthy.'* (Monologue)
2. 'No stranger to controversy, Dr Bryce has long sought to make his name – and his fortune – in this field.' (News report)
3. 'I nodded, looking around. I took more of an interest in my surroundings.' (First-person narrative)

● Ask the children: *What clues in the text showed where each quotation came from?* (1: Informal colloquialisms; commentary rather than sequential events. 2: Value judgements in third-person text; formal wording; emotive use of words. 3: Description of sequential events.)
● Ask the children to re-read Chapters 13 and 14, asking them to notice the structure and use of language, and how it changes.
● Provide the children with photocopiable page 17 to complete with reference to the book.

> **Differentiation**
> **For older/more confident learners:** Challenge the children to find a fourth style of writing (Cam's poem) and supply a description and quotation.
> **For younger/less confident learners:** Provide quotations and statements for the children to sort and stick onto their worksheets.

Plot locked in characters

> **Objective:** To make notes on and use evidence from across a text to explain events or ideas.
> **What you need:** Copies of *Pig-heart Boy*, writing materials.

What to do

● Ask the children what the story is about, also reading aloud the back-cover blurb. Ask if there are any underlying storylines about the characters. List the children's suggestions.
● Point out that all the relationships are interconnected and are affected by events and moods, hopes and fears, health and wealth. Explain that the characters' personalities and interaction are essential and integral to the plot.
● Divide the children into groups, allocating one character from the book to each group. Provide each group with a large sheet of paper, with the character's name written in the centre.

Ask each group to create a spider chart, centred round the character's name. At the end of the radial lines, the children should write adjectives describing the character, supported by textual evidence, quotations and references, including page numbers.
● Invite the groups to present their findings to the class, explaining their choices with reference to the text.

> **Differentiation**
> **For older/more confident learners:** Challenge the children to explain how the story is enhanced by the personalities of each character, and how these affect the outcome of different events.
> **For younger/less confident learners:** Write appropriate adjectives on the spider chart and point the children towards specific sections of text to search for evidence.

Plot, character and setting

Hitting the roof!

> **Objective:** To appraise a text quickly, deciding on its value, quality or usefulness.
> **What you need:** Copies of *Pig-heart Boy*, extract 3, writing materials.

What to do

● Re-read Extract 3 together. Ask how the author makes the character use language to dramatic effect: *Why the short sentences at the opening?* (Breathless; matter-of-fact.) *What about the use of figurative expressions?* (These add vivid emphasis to Cam's feelings.) *What is the purpose of the repetition of the word 'thousands'?* (To impress and emphasise.)
● Draw attention to rhetorical questions and colloquialisms. Invite the children to look for similar expressions within the same chapter.
● Ask what evidence there is that Cameron had calmed down or amended his view before and after talking to the webcam. Discuss why Cameron wants no dinner, but later relents.
● Ask: *What can we infer is the effect on Cameron of talking to the webcam?* (It releases his feelings; it helps him to calm down and take stock; it helps him to recognise his parents' point of view.)

> **Differentiation**
> **For older/more confident learners:** Challenge the children to write a few paragraphs explaining how, when and why talking to the webcam helps Cameron, throughout the whole story.
> **For younger/less confident learners:** Invite the children to write in speech bubbles Cameron's strongest feelings as expressed in Chapter 17. These may be direct or reworded quotations, or new speeches inferred from his behaviour.

When fact meets fiction

> **Objective:** To appraise a text quickly, deciding on its value, quality or usefulness.
> **What you need:** Copies of *Pig-heart Boy*, photocopiable page 18, writing materials.
> **Cross-curricular link:** History

What to do

● Explain that when *Pig-heart Boy* was first published, research into xenotransplantation was at its height – it seemed to be a viable option. Other research, plus increased knowledge of DNA, has since overtaken this idea (such as the use of human stem-cells).
● Ask the children: *How can authors write with authority about such subjects?* (They usually search medical journals and news archives.) *How can readers check the reliability of the factual content of such novels?* (Through research.)
● Hand out copies of photocopiable page 18. Invite the children to underline statements that reinforce information learned from the novel.
● Ask the children to draw and complete a two-column table of 'facts', under the headings of '*Pig-heart Boy* (fiction)' and 'Article (non-fiction)'.
● Discuss how differently the facts are presented, such as through dialogue (fiction) or in statements (non-fiction). Ask the children: *In what ways do both sources consider the pros and cons of such a procedure?*

> **Differentiation**
> **For older/more confident learners:** Challenge the children to conduct further research, assessing sources for reliability and usefulness.
> **For younger/less confident learners:** Ask the children to list the pros and cons of transplanting a pig's heart into a human, marking each point with F (fiction) or NF (non-fiction) (or both), depending on support in the novel and/or article.

Plot, character and setting

Weighty words

- Re-read Chapter 5 of *Pig-heart Boy.*
- Read the following statements. Tick one box next to each. Explain your answers with reference to the text. (You can use quotations from the book.)

1. At first, Marlon thinks Cameron must be mad even to think about having a pig's heart implanted.
Why? (Explain your choice of tick-box.)

☐ True   ☐ False

_____

_____

2. Cameron trusts Marlon completely.
Why?

☐ True   ☐ False

_____

_____

3. Cameron rates his chance of leading a normal life above any other consideration.
Why?

☐ True   ☐ False

_____

_____

4. Marlon is angry when Cameron makes a joke of the proposed operation because he is concerned for his friend.
Why?

☐ True   ☐ False

_____

_____

Plot, character and setting

Communicating views

- An author can show her views through her characters' behaviour.
- At times **we can see** what Malorie Blackman thinks through a character. Often **we can infer** more, through characters' words and actions, about their feelings or thoughts – and the author's view of human situations.
- Look at these examples of communication, or lack of communication, between characters. Decide what **we can see** and what **we can infer**.
- Add more examples from Chapters 7, 8 and 9 of *Pig-heart Boy*.

Chapter	Text quoted	We can see…	We can infer…
7	No one said a thing that wasn't a monosyllable.	Cam and his parents were hardly talking to each other.	They were lost for words; deep in thought about the whole situation; not ready to share their feelings.
7	Mum flicked my chin.		

Plot, character and setting

Style and structure

- In the boxes below, write a brief description of each style of writing. Mention layout and font, tense, person, use of language, and direct speech.
- Under each box, write a direct quotation from Chapters 13 or 14 of *Pig-heart Boy* that demonstrates the style.

---

1. Story narrative

Quotation: _____

_____

---

2. News report

Quotation: _____

_____

---

3. Monologue or soliloquy

Quotation: _____

_____

When fact meets fiction

Abridged from an article titled 'Pigged out' from *The Economist* (January 22nd 1998).

An infinite supply of organs would be a transplant surgeon's dream. And some surgeons think they have found a way to make that dream come true: by husbanding pigs not for their chops but for their hearts, livers, lungs and even their neurons. This could instantly solve the vexing shortage of spare human parts – commodities that, in tribute to the surgeons' success, are in increasingly short supply. Yet, such a solution carries the risk of disease. For such 'xenotransplants' would be an open invitation for hitherto unknown animal diseases to transfer themselves to people.

Transplant patients are already at risk from diseases. Organs from corpses are not always healthy, and the drugs that patients must take to prevent rejection of their new organs make them vulnerable to infections that those with robust immune systems do not usually get. But these illnesses are, at least, known human illnesses, and are unlikely to unleash an epidemic in the general population. Animal diseases are not so predictable. Many viruses are harmless in their regular hosts (and therefore difficult or impossible to detect) but devastating if they switch to a new one.

Most of those interested in xenotransplantation are considering pigs, rather than baboons or chimpanzees, because pigs are easier and cheaper to rear, and because harvesting pigs for organs is thought to pose fewer ethical difficulties. But many of them also harbour an erroneous belief that pigs, unlike primates, pose a small risk of passing infections to people. This belief rests on two (contradictory) pillars: first, that parasites adapted to pigs would have a hard time adapting to humans, and, second, that because pigs and people have lived together for so long, any parasites likely to switch have already done so. Neither argument is cause for comfort. Little is understood about how diseases swap between species, or the conditions that make it easy for them to do so.

Talk about it

Do all questions need answers?

> **Objective:** To use and explore different question types and different ways words are used, including in formal and informal contexts.
> **What you need:** Copies of *Pig-heart Boy*, writing materials.

What to do
● Explain to the children that Cameron is full of questions – some voiced, some unspoken. List the following examples from Chapter 3:
  ● 'A pig-heart boy? What on earth was Mum talking about?'
  ● 'So you want me to have a pig's heart?'
  ● 'Why didn't you tell me before?'
  ● 'How could I forget?'
Let the children decide which examples are: spoken; require an answer; have a finite answer; need a complicated, infinite response; are rhetorical. Are some internal dialogue?

● Ask the children to read Chapter 4. In groups of three or four, encourage them to role play Cam, Dr Bryce, Mum and/or Dad, scripting the questions and responses that occur. Tell the children that they may paraphrase and add questions of their own.
● As they prepare to act the scene, challenge the children to include different kinds of question. Internal dialogue cab be spoken as an aside to the audience, such as: 'Have they noticed I'm here?'

> **Differentiation**
> **For older/more confident learners:** Encourage the children to use body language and facial acting to help show the nature of the questions and the level of emotion.
> **For younger/less confident learners:** Create a script with the children, colour-coding their respective parts for ease of reference when they read (or improvise) as appropriate.

Discussing and deciding

> **Objective:** To use the techniques of dialogic talk to explore ideas, topics or issues.
> **What you need:** Copies of *Pig-heart Boy*, writing materials.

What to do
● In the book, the viewpoints of some of the characters gradually change. Ask the children when this happens, and why. For example:
  ● Cam's mum – against the whole pig's heart idea at first; later in favour.
  ● Julie – initially caring for and about Cam; prejudiced against him once she knows about the operation.
● Demonstrate from these and other examples how viewpoints can change over time, with increased knowledge and experience.
● Select an issue raised in the novel, such as breeding animals for human 'spare parts'. Discuss how genetic engineering compares with breeding for meat. How might this alter opinion, due to moral and/or health considerations?
● Suggest that the children use hypothesis: 'If… then…' (such as: 'If I were in Cam's position, then…').
● Encourage the children to listen open-mindedly to views opposing their own, and to share and expand on ideas raised.
● Invite individuals to sum up the discussion in writing, explaining viewpoints expressed, and

> **Differentiation**
> **For older/more confident learners:** Challenge the children to write an argument in favour of a belief that is directly opposed to their own, in order to help them to see a different viewpoint.
> **For younger/less confident learners:** Help the children to express their summary in simple sentences. 'John thinks… because…. I (dis)agree because…'

Talk about it

The language of conflict

Objective: To consider examples of conflict and resolution, exploring the language used.
What you need: Copies of *Pig-heart Boy*, photocopiable page 22, writing materials.

What to do
- Read aloud some examples of conflict between characters. For example: Chapter 18, from 'I'm sorry. I'm sorry. *I'm sorry!*' to 'D'you *grab*?!'
- Ask the children what they notice about the dialogue. Is it logical, reasoned debate? What do the exclamation marks and italics indicate? (Shouting.) Invite the children to analyse how aggression is evident. (Condescending expressions; use of 'gunfire' rhetorical repetition of D'you… d'you… d'you….')
- Invite the children to find and note further examples, analysing how effectively the dialogue portrays anger and conflict.
- Hand out copies of photocopiable page 22 and ask the children to complete it.
- Encourage the children to look, in contrast, for the language of conciliation, such as when Cam and Marlon make up. Ask: *How does the language differ?*
- Divide the class into groups of six or seven. Appoint one child to role play Cameron and the others to divide into his supporters and critics. Tell the group to improvise a scene of conflict. Begin by one critic name-calling 'Pig-heart boy!' Develop this into an improvised argument for or against Cameron.

Differentiation
For older/more confident learners: Challenge the children to script a conflict dialogue that could have taken place during break time (on Cam's post-operative return to school).
For younger/less confident learners: Help the children to find dialogue directly from the text to launch their improvisation.

Cam-corder!

Objective: To devise a performance, considering how to adapt it for a specific audience.
What you need: Copies of *Pig-heart Boy*, an enlarged copy of Extract 3 (page 10), lined writing paper, different-coloured pens or pencils.
Cross-curricular link: Drama.

What to do
- Display Extract 3. Explain that this is just one of many monologues by Cam in the book. Suggest that it is like hearing the character's thoughts.
- Explain that Cameron is facing a camera, knowing that one day Alex will watch the video. Ask the children to imagine that they are 'performing' to a camcorder. Discuss the importance of facial expression and gesture.
- Invite suggestions on how to stage the monologue in the persona of Cameron talking to Alex. Demonstrate annotating the text: underlining stressed words, adding marginal notes (thumbs up, point to self and so on), marking pauses with " or /. Ask the children if they think the orator should be seated – perhaps standing at times.
- Ask the children how Cam might change his tone of voice.
- Invite each child to choose a monologue and copy it out on lined paper. Advise them to write on alternate lines, leaving those in between for annotation in a contrasting colour.

Differentiation
For older/more confident learners: Challenge the children to learn their chosen script by heart and perform it to the class.
For younger/less confident learners: Allow the children to work in twos or threes, breaking up the chosen text into smaller chunks.

Talk about it

Defending the indefensible

> **Objective:** To present a spoken argument, sequencing points logically, defending views with evidence and making use of persuasive language.
> **What you need:** Copies of *Pig-heart Boy*, photocopiable page 23.

What to do
● Ask the children how they would feel if they told their best friend a secret, and that friend broke their trust.
● Ask the children if it is possible to defend the indefensible, listing, with the children's help, some of the effects that Marlon's breaking Cameron's trust had on him and his family:
  ● home under siege
  ● lies and half-truths spread across the papers
  ● impact on friendships
  ● the stranger's assault
  ● daily deliveries of hate mail.
● Ask the children to re-read a passages relating to one of the consequences of the story being released to the press. In doing so, ask them to choose one character who behaved unkindly towards Cameron, either unintentionally (as Marlon), through ignorance and fear (as Julie), or with malice (as the woman attacker and the letter-writers).
● Provide each child with a copy of photocopiable page 23. Challenge the children to plan and practise a spoken defence, justifying their behaviour, using the planning sheet to note and sequence their argument.

> **Differentiation**
> **For older/more confident learners:** After delivering their planned defence, challenge the children to take the hot-seat to answer questions, in role.
> **For younger/less confident learners:** Ask an adult to work with the children to help them to locate textual evidence to support their chosen character's viewpoint.

This house believes

> **Objective:** To participate in a whole-class debate, using the conventions and language of debate, including standard English.
> **What you need:** Copies of *Pig-heart Boy*, photocopiable page 24.

What to do
● Explain that formal debate has conventions in the way and order in which an opinion is argued and counter-argued. It begins when one faction, called for debating purposes a 'house', makes a proposal. The proposal sets out a belief based on a considered thought process. Both houses' speakers take it in turns to speak, with a chairman to oversee proceedings and sum up.
● Hand out copies of photocopiable page 24. The sheet shows in which order the participants speak, and the purpose of each speech.
● Invite the class to choose an area of debate, based on issues raised in *Pig-heart Boy*. Divide the class into two groups, appointing speakers and a chairperson. Speakers can make notes on their photocopiable sheets.
● Carry out the debate, asking non-participants to vote according to the conviction of the speakers rather than on the issue itself. Explain that they must consider: the speakers' use of persuasive language; their quality of reasoning sequence; their ability to build on points raised; their clarity of oral delivery. (The audience could award each speaker points out of 10 in each of these areas.)

> **Differentiation**
> **For older/more confident learners:** Challenge the children to hold their debate in front of another class, to increase their confidence-building experience.
> **For younger/less confident learners:** Encourage the children to write brief notes on numbered cards to help them to keep track of the sequence of speaking.

The language of conflict

Chapter (+ page number)	Quotation (+ speaker)	Notes
Chapter 3 (17)	'Stop it! Stop it, both of you!' (Cam)	Use of ! means shouting. Repetition (Stop it!)

- My ideas for dialogue for Cameron's friends and supporters:

- My ideas for dialogue for Cameron's critics:

Defending the indefensible

- As you fill in the gaps below, remember that you are putting together an argument to explain and justify your actions, *as a character in the book.*
- Remember, not everyone will agree with your opinions and behaviour, so you must use *persuasive language.*
- Your argument will be stronger if you take care over the sequence of points that you make. It may help if you *number these.*

> NOTE: I am thinking with my chosen character's mindset – not with my own!

My character is _____

What I think about Cameron's pig's heart transplant:

_____

_____

What I have done that has affected Cameron's life and his family:

_____

_____

Why I have done this – how I defend my actions:

_____

_____

_____

_____

Debater's guide

Proposal to be debated:

This house believes _____

_____

| pro |

| 1st proposer's main points: |

| con |

| 1st opposer's responses to 1st proposer's main points (also adding new arguments): |

| 2nd proposer's responses to 1st opposer's arguments (also expanding on 1st proposer's main points): |

| 2nd opposer's responses to 2nd proposer's arguments (also expanding on 1st opposer's main points): |

1. Chairman sums up:
   (a) What the house believes – and, briefly, why.
   (b) What the opposers believe – and, briefly, why.
2. Reminds the audience that, in this debate, they are voting for the house that argued their case most convincingly, clearly and persuasively.
3. Counts votes and declares which house wins the debate.

SCHOLASTIC
www.scholastic.co.uk

Get writing

Some choice. No choice.

Objectives: To create multi-layered texts, including use of hyperlinks and linked web pages; in non-narrative, to establish, balance and maintain viewpoints.
What you need: Copies of *Pig-heart Boy*, writing materials, photocopiable page 28.
Cross-curricular links: ICT.

What to do
● Gain agreement that Cameron has a difficult decision to make. Quote from Chapter 1: 'If I don't take a breath I'll burst. If I do take a breath, I'll drown. Some choice. No choice.' Although this relates directly to Cam's underwater experience, ask how it might reflect his whole life. (If he has no operation, he will die; if he does, he may still die.)
● Ask the children to re-read Chapters 4,
5 and 6, making notes on photocopiable page 28. Explain that 'pros and cons' means that making a decision involves weighing up advantages against disadvantages.
● Working from their notes, and with close reference to the text, ask the children to adopt Cam's persona to design a blog explaining how he reached his decision – with sequential updates as he learns more and works towards his decision and its aftermath.

Differentiation
For older/more confident learners: Challenge the children to create links to information sites on the subject.
For younger/less confident learners: Ask the children to write 'before' and 'after' lists relating to Cam's restricted life without the operation, and his potentially improved life after it.

Life lessons

Objective: To select words and language, drawing on their knowledge of literary features and formal and informal writing.
What you need: Copies of *Pig-heart Boy*, photocopiable page 29, writing materials.
Cross-curricular link: ICT.

What to do
● Ask if anyone can remember Cam's phrase to describe his advice to Alex. (Life lessons, in the eponymous Chapter 11.) Re-read this chapter together. Explain that Cam's wallpaper analogy is used widely: 'papering over the cracks'. Can the children find other figurative expressions? ('Gnawing in the pit of my stomach'; 'a bombshell of her own'; 'a fly on the wall'.)
● Discern what 'life lesson' Cam is teaching here. (Mum and Dad know a lot, but not everything. They don't like to think their child might know more.)
● Ask what Cam means by his 'newsreader
voice'. (Formal language, suited to a formal presentation.)
● Hand out copies of photocopiable page 29. Explain to the children that they are going to plan a short leaflet of advice for younger siblings. Explain that under the main heading, 'Life lessons', each new topic should have a subheading.
● Advise the children to use formal language in an introductory paragraph. Encourage them to use figurative expressions in their advice.
● Allow time for the children to transfer their draft to a computer, formatting it into a single-fold 4-page booklet from one A4 sheet.

Differentiation
For older/more confident learners: Ask the children to present the text, reading it aloud to a partner, to help ascertain if it can be improved (for example, on clarity and vocabulary).
For younger/less confident learners: Act as scribe for the children, writing down their ideas for them.

Get writing

Stories with style

> **Objective:** To experiment with different narrative forms and styles to write their own stories.
> **What you need:** Copies of *Pig-heart Boy*, writing materials.

What to do

● Inviting the children's suggestions, list the different styles of writing that Malorie Blackman incorporates in *Pig-heart Boy*: monologue, narrative (including dialogue), news report, poem, letter, internal dialogue/soliloquy, interview.

● Remind the children that there are several considerations when planning a story: character, setting and plot. Often, as in *Pig-heart Boy*, there are theme(s): loyalty, ethics, morals, relationships, and so on.

● Ask the children to plan an outline for a story. There must be one main problem for the protagonist (or hero) which, to be overcome, involves a difficult decision. For example, a child needs money for food – should he/she steal ?

● Invite the children, when they have planned their story with a moral or ethical dilemma, to decide how to tell it. Challenge them to include at least one other style of writing within their narrative.

> **Differentiation**
> **For older/more confident learners:** Challenge the children to write a longer story in short chapters.
> **For younger/less confident learners:** Let the children work with a partner, using the example above as their outline story plan.

Spin-offs

> **Objective:** To reflect independently and critically on own writing and edit and improve it.
> **What you need:** Copies of *Pig-heart Boy*, writing materials, enlarged copy of Extract 2 (page 9).

What to do

● Together, re-read Extract 2. Invite descriptions of style, language and tone. (Sensational, provocative.) Ask the children: *How might readers react?* (Shock, (dis)belief, condemnation, sympathy, (mis)understanding.) Point out that some suggestions are opposites. Ask: *Can we infer that the article will elicit strong opinions?*

● Suggest that the subject matter alone is controversial. Then highlight: emotive words and phrases, such as 'dramatic' and 'time running out'; conjecture, not fact, such as 'a new wave of transplants'; judgemental phrases, such as 'remarkably cool' and 'no stranger to controversy'.

● Together, look again at the hate-mail letter (Chapter 20). Explain that it results directly from the news item. Ask the children: *Does the writer know Cam, his parents and the doctor? Does the letter allude to any informed source?* Discuss the concept of strangers forming judgements without access to the facts.

● Assuming people are entitled to their opinion, ask: *What would be a suitable platform to express an opinion, however ill-informed?* (A newspaper letters page, for example.)

● Invite the children to write two contrasting 'letters to the editor' in response to the article, one condoning and one condemning Cam's treatment, creating different author personae.

● Encourage the children to redraft their letters wearing their 'Newspaper editor's hat' (lengthy letters get edited!). What unnecessary words can be removed? Can anything be rephrased to be more concise or more strongly expressed?

> **Differentiation**
> **For older/more confident learners:** Challenge the children to revise their letters to a word count.
> **For younger/less confident learners:** Help the children to adapt the LEPAR letter, addressing it 'Dear Editor'.

Get writing

Eulogies, poems and tributes

> **Objective:** To integrate words, images and sounds imaginatively for different purposes.
> **What you need:** Copies of *Pig-heart Boy*, writing materials.

What to do

● Ask the children to make notes on Nan, reading especially closely Chapters 20, 26 and 27. These should cover Nan's character, her sayings and her relationship with Cam.

● Encourage the children to voice how they think Cam feels when Nan dies, sharing opinions and quoting from the text. Some may want to share their own experiences of personal loss.

● Explain that, when someone you love dies, it often helps to talk about them. Sometimes people turn to writing, music or art to express their feelings. They may write an obituary (a formal tribute) or a eulogy (such as might be read out at a funeral) or a poem.

● Ask the children to 'put themselves in Cameron's shoes' and choose their form of written tribute to his grandmother. They could write a poem 'For Nan', modelling it on Cameron's poem in Chapter 9, paraphrasing recurring lines, such as 'Missing my nan, wanting her back'.

● Encourage the children to listen for rhythm and cadence in their words, whether prose or poetry. Invite them to consider how they could present their finished piece, integrating their words with music and/or images.

> **Differentiation**
> **For older/more confident learners:** Challenge the children to direct their friends to form a Kelsey family tableau – Cam, Mum, Dad and Nan – as a backdrop to a reading or recitation of their writing.
> **For younger/less confident learners:** Help the children to create a fact-file on Nan, inventing dates of birth and death; lived in Bradford; mother to Cathy; mother in law to…; grandmother to…, and so on.

What next?

> **Objective:** To use paragraphs to achieve pace and emphasis.
> **What you need:** Copies of *Pig-heart Boy*, photocopiable page 30, writing materials.

● At the end of the book, readers are left with an optimistic view. Cameron is waiting for his baby sibling to be born and is determined to be there when he/she arrives. The last chapter is Cameron's final webcam recording.

● Ask the children to consider what might happen next. Answers could include Cameron's dying before or after the baby is born, living just a few more years, or living long into healthy adulthood. Establish that the open ending leaves it for the reader to decide.

● Remind the children that Cameron is 13 years old in the novel. Ask them to imagine that Alex gets to watch his recordings when he/she reaches 13. The children must each decide for themselves whether Alex is a girl or a boy.

● Ask them to imagine, for the purposes of this exercise, that when Alex watches the recordings he/she is alone, just as Cam was when he taped them.

● Hand out copies of photocopiable page 30. Ask the children to write the text of Alex's own webcam monologue, addressed to his/her (late or absent) older brother, Cameron.

> **Differentiation**
> **For older/more confident learners:** Challenge the children to redraft their text, making sure that pace varies, ending on an optimistic note.
> **For younger/less confident learners:** Act as a scribe for the children as they voice their monologue in the persona of Alex.

Some choice. No choice.

- Re-read Chapters 4 to 6 of *Pig-heart Boy*.
- Make notes on how and why Cameron made his decision.

At the opening of the story Cameron's life is severely **restricted**.
If he does nothing he **will soon die**.
If he receives a xenotransplant he might live a **normal**, and **longer**, **life**.

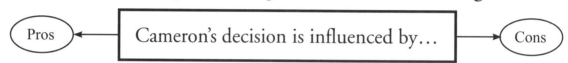

Pros ← Cameron's decision is influenced by… → Cons

- Add to the pros and cons that Cameron has to weigh up in his mind.

Pros	&	Cons
If successful, will live longer and be able to do sports.		Will need to have operation with inherent dangers.

At the end of Chapter 6, Cam says: 'I looked at Mum, and reached my decision…'

- What was Cam's decision, and why?

_____

_____

Life lessons

- Plan the content of a leaflet titled 'Life lessons' for a younger sibling.
- Introductory paragraph (use formal language to explain the leaflet's purpose):

_____

_____

_____

_____

_____

- Give each new topic a subheading to say the area of life the lesson covers.
- Make notes for each topic using informal language, such as figurative expressions.
- Use the following subheadings, and think of more of your own:
- PARENTS

_____

_____

- SCHOOL

_____

_____

- LEISURE TIME

_____

_____

-

_____

-

_____

Get writing

What next?

*Hello, Cameron. My name is Alex Kelsey. I am your brother/sister.
(delete one) I am 13 years old, just as you were when you made those recordings
for me. I have just watched them all.*

Plan what you want to say to next. Start a new paragraph for each part of
your monologue. Some suggestions have been made for you.

- **Paragraph 1:** (You might thank Cam for his life lessons and tell him what
  you found helpful or interesting, or what you admire about him.)

- **Paragraph 2:** (Maybe, something about your own life and what is
  happening. How is it different from Cameron's? What is the same?)

- **Paragraph 3:** Something you are planning for the future – friendships?
  school? career plans for when you leave school?

Assessment

Assessment advice

The first-person narrative of *Pig-heart Boy* will help children to identify with the central character, Cameron, and relate to his predicament. As the character's thoughts and feelings are shared throughout the story, they will gain understanding of what is involved in the decision-making process of a life-changing situation. They will also observe different perspectives (of parents, children, doctors, teachers, friends and enemies). Discussing the issues that arise, from the peripheral playground bullying to the central heart transplant, will enable children to explore their own prejudices, fears and feelings, and examine the possibilities of adapting viewpoints in the light of knowledge.

Some children may have first-hand experience of losing a close member of their family or of invasive medical procedures. The book may ring more or less true to them but, either way, they may draw from some strategies that Cameron employs to cope with his situation, such as talking to somebody, writing a poem, setting themselves tasks and goals. There is ample scope, during the study of this text, to observe children's levels of empathy with the subject matter and characters, which may be exploited to help children to increase their own self-knowledge and confidence.

The book, being fiction, allows for objective discussion, adding safe distance to share personal thoughts. Allow ample time for debate, encouraging children to listen to each other's points of view, follow up and build on others' observations, and develop logical arguments to support opinions.

It's simple really

> **Objective:** To assess understanding of underlying themes, causes and points of view.
> **What you need:** Photocopiable page 32, copies of *Pig-heart Boy* (optional), writing materials.

What to do

● The assessment sheet (photocopiable page 32) is designed to be used when the children have finished reading and studying the book. Most children should be able to answer the questions based on their memory and understanding of the novel, without the book in front of them. This also encourages children to use their own words rather than copying directly from the narrative.

● Some questions are a simple test of the child's knowledge and understanding. For example, question 1 simply assesses whether children understand the term 'narrator' as distinct from 'author'. Others, such as the final question, require a broader appreciation, and inferential discernment, of the themes explored in the book.

● Explain that you want as full an answer as possible. In some questions, there may be more than one aspect to consider to support their answer. For example, question 2: Cameron does not join in the Daredevil Dive game because (a) he can't physically compete with any chance of winning, and (b) he knows the strain on his heart could kill him. Either answer is correct; both give a fuller response.

● Provide each child with a copy of photocopiable page 32, explaining that they must write their answers according to what they think, without discussion with others.

● Listen to the children's explanation of their answers. Look for evidence of inferential understanding, such as recognition that Julie's response is influenced by her mother.

It's simple really

1. Who is the narrator in *Pig-heart Boy*?

_____

2. Why does Cameron not join in the Daredevil Dive game?

_____

3. Why does he not want his parents to know he's been swimming?

_____

4. Give two arguments that Dr Bryce uses to convince the Kelseys that the transplant has a good chance of success.

_____

_____

5. When Marlon says 'It's simple really' is Cam's 'catchphrase', what does he mean?

_____

_____

6. How does his catchphrase help Cameron to make his decision?

_____

_____

7. When Cam returns to school, Andrew says he has changed. Which of the following words does he use to describe Cameron? (Underline two of the options).

      pushy   confident   arrogant

8. Why did Julie no longer want to have anything to do with Cameron?

_____

_____

9. How did Cameron's use of the camcorder help him to cope with events?

_____

_____